Oxford Read and Discover

3

Wonderful Water

Cheryl Palin

Contents

T0344571

OXFORD

UNIVERSITY PRESS

OXFORD
UNIVERSITY PRESS

Great Clarendon Street, Oxford OX2 6DP

Oxford University Press is a department of the University of Oxford. It furthers the University's objective of excellence in research, scholarship, and education by publishing worldwide in

Oxford New York

Auckland Cape Town Dar es Salaam Hong Kong Karachi Kuala Lumpur Madrid Melbourne Mexico City Nairobi New Delhi Shanghai Taipei Toronto

With offices in

Argentina Austria Brazil Chile Czech Republic France Greece Guatemala Hungary Italy Japan Poland Portugal Singapore South Korea Switzerland Thailand Turkey Ukraine Vietnam

OXFORD and OXFORD ENGLISH are registered trade marks of Oxford University Press in the UK and in certain other countries

© Oxford University Press 2010

The moral rights of the author have been asserted

Database right Oxford University Press (maker)

First published 2010

2023
31

ISBN: 978 0 19 464376 4

An Audio Pack containing this book and an Audio download is also available, ISBN: 978 0 19 402189 0

This book is also available as an e-Book, ISBN: 978 0 19 410880 5.

An accompanying Activity Book is also available ISBN: 978 0 19 464386 3

Printed in China

This book is printed on paper from certified and well-managed sources.

ACKNOWLEDGEMENTS

Illustrations by: Tom Hughes pp.14 (human body), 34; Alan Rowe pp.26, 30, 32, 33, 35, 36, 37, 38, 40, 41, 42, 43, 44, 46, 47; Martin Sanders pp.4, 8, 25, 28, 29; Gary Swift pp.7, 9, 14 (cartoon), 15, 19, 20.

The Publishers would also like to thank the following for their kind permission to reproduce photographs and other copyright material: Alamy pp.4, 17 (Brandon Cole Marine Photography), 18 (Images of Africa Photobank); Getty Images pp.3 (glacier/Michael Blann/Iconica), 5 (Russell Kord), 15 (Finn Roberts), 21 (Kazuhiro Nogi/AFP), 27 (glacier/Michael Blann/Iconica); iStockPhoto pp.3 (river and mountains/Matt Tilghman, ice/Evgeny Terentev, clouds/Rotofrank, beach/Benjamin Goode, water vapour/Ben Renard-Wiart), 7 (Tatiana Popova), 9 (Stockcam), 10 (shower/Warwick Lister-Kaye, bathroom/Kristian Septimus Krogh, bath/Slobo Mitic, brushing teeth/Yulia Saponova), 11 (washing machine/Oman Mirzaie, laundry/Don Nichols), 12 (Debra Feinman), 22 (Iofoto), 23 (polluted water/Brian Humek, clean water/Maksym Dragunov), 27 (river and mountains/Matt Tilghman, clouds/Rotofrank, sapling/Kais Tolmats, cave/Tatiana Popova); Nature Picture Library pp.16 (Alex Mustard); NASA Images pp.6 (Lake Superior); Oxford University Press pp.6 (River Nile/Shutterstock), 13 (Shutterstock), 27 (River Nile/Shutterstock); Shutterstock pp.19 (Bryan Hall), 20 (Roschetzky Photography).

Introduction

Water is all around us. We have liquid water in rivers and oceans. We have frozen water in ice and glaciers, and we have water vapor in clouds and steam. Water is very important.

liquid water frozen water water vapor

How many oceans are there?
What is the biggest ocean animal?
How much water do we use to take a bath?
What percent (%) of our body is water?

Discover!

Now read and discover
more about wonderful water!

Salt Water

About 70% of Earth is covered with water. Most of the water is in the oceans. There are five oceans – the Pacific Ocean, the Atlantic Ocean, the Indian Ocean, the Southern Ocean, and the Arctic Ocean. The largest ocean is the Pacific Ocean. It's 156 million square kilometers. It's about 15 times bigger than the USA!

Earth

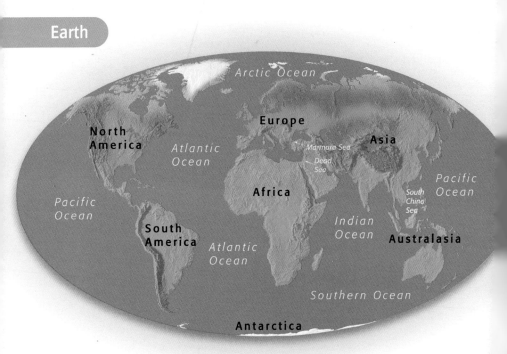

There are also many seas on Earth.
The largest sea is the South China Sea.
It's 3 million square kilometers. One of the
smallest seas is the Marmara Sea. It's only
about 11,000 square kilometers.

All the water in the oceans and seas is
salt water.

Floating in the Dead Sea

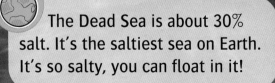

Discover! The Dead Sea is about 30%
salt. It's the saltiest sea on Earth.
It's so salty, you can float in it!

Go to pages 24–25 for activities.

2 Fresh Water

About 3% of the water on Earth is fresh water. Most of this fresh water is frozen. It's ice. It's in glaciers or polar ice caps.

Some of the fresh water is in lakes and rivers. One of the biggest lakes on Earth is Lake Superior in North America. It's about 82,000 square kilometers. The longest river on Earth is the River Nile in Africa. It's about 6,700 kilometers long.

River Nile

Lake Superior

Some of the fresh water is in the sky. It's in the clouds and the rain. Some of the water is in the soil, in rocks, or under the ground in caves.

Discover!

Most of Earth is covered with water, but only about 1% is fresh water that we can drink. The rest is salt water or ice.

Go to pages 26–27 for activities.

The Water Cycle

Do you know where water comes from? When it rains, water falls from the sky. This is called precipitation. Rainwater goes into streams. Stream water goes into rivers. River water goes into seas and oceans.

When it's sunny, the ocean water gets warm. Some water goes up into the sky. This is called evaporation. The water in the sky makes clouds. Then it rains again. This is called the water cycle.

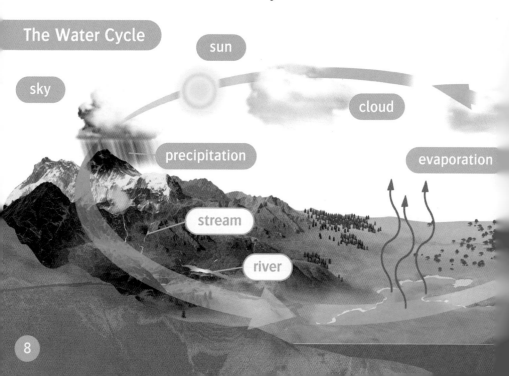

The Water Cycle

sun

sky

cloud

precipitation

evaporation

stream

river

Discover!

We're lucky to have water in our homes! About one billion people don't have clean water in their homes.

Most of the water we use comes from rivers and reservoirs. Clean water goes through pipes to our homes.

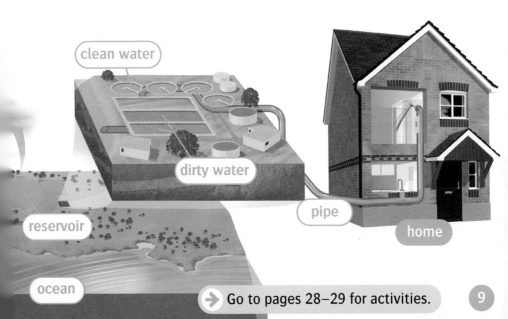

clean water

dirty water

pipe

reservoir

home

ocean

Go to pages 28–29 for activities.

Water at Home

We use a lot of water at home. We drink water and we cook with water. We also use water for washing.

We use about 80 liters of water when we take a bath. We use about 27 liters of water when we take a shower. We use water to brush our teeth and we also need water to flush the toilet. We use about 9 liters of water every time we flush.

We use water to wash and clean other things, too. We wash the dishes with water. We wash clothes with water. We wash and clean everything in the house with water!

Go to pages 30–31 for activities.

Water Activities

We use a lot of water outside the home. We need water for the food we eat. Meat comes from animals, and animals drink water. Fruits and vegetables also need water to grow. We need water to travel. We can travel by ship and by boat. We can also make power with water. Hydroelectricity is electricity made from water.

Making Electricity

We have fun with water. We like to go to the beach in the summer. We also like to visit rivers and lakes.

Lots of sports need water. Sailing, surfing, swimming, waterskiing, and diving all use water. Which water sports do you like?

→ Go to pages 32–33 for activities.

We Need Water

The human body contains lots of water. Our body is about 70% water. Our brain is about 85% water and our bones are about 33% water. Water is very important for the human body. We can live for four weeks without food, but we can't live for more than about three days without water!

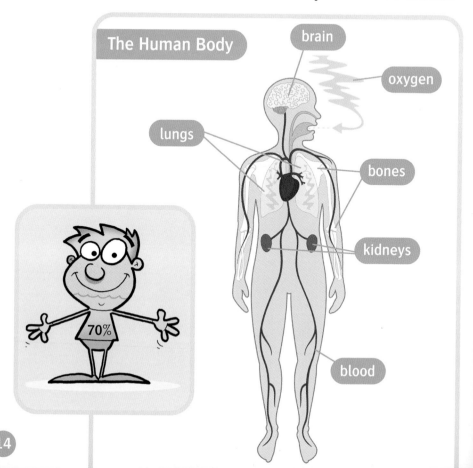

The Human Body

brain

oxygen

lungs

bones

kidneys

blood

70%

We need to drink about eight glasses of water every day. We need to drink even more water when we play sports and when it's hot. We need water because it keeps our blood healthy. Our blood is about 50% water. Blood takes food to different parts of our body. It takes oxygen from our lungs to other parts of our body, too.

Discover!

If we don't drink water, our body gets dehydrated. If we're dehydrated, our kidneys and our brain don't work. Then we get very sick.

Go to pages 34–35 for activities.

Ocean Animals

Lots of animals live in water. Some animals live in salt water. They live in seas and oceans.

The biggest ocean animal is the blue whale. It can be more than 30 meters long and 200 metric tons. It eats very small ocean animals called krill. It can eat 4 metric tons of krill in a day! Blue whales live in most of the oceans.

Discover!

The blue whale is the biggest animal on Earth. It can be as big as 25 elephants.

x 25
= 1 blue whale

A Jellyfish

Many other animals live in salt water. There are sharks and lots of other fish. All ocean animals need water. Water gives them food and oxygen.

Jellyfish are not fish – they are invertebrates. They don't have a skeleton. They need water to support their bodies.

Go to pages 36–37 for activities.

Other Animals

Some animals live in fresh water. They live in rivers and lakes. Fish, frogs, beavers, and ducks live in fresh water.

A Nile Crocodile

Big animals also live in fresh water. The Nile crocodile lives in rivers and lakes in Africa. When large animals come to drink, it pulls them under the water and eats them!

Land animals need water, too. They drink water. In the African savannah, animals, like zebras, giraffes, and elephants, come to the waterhole to drink. The savannah can be very hot and dry, and these animals cannot live without water.

Discover!

Hippos need water to keep their skin healthy. They stay in water all day to keep cool. If they don't have water, they get sunburnt!

Go to pages 38–39 for activities.

9 Too Much Water

Floods can happen when there is too much rain. Rivers and lakes become very full. Floods can also happen when there are very big waves in the ocean.

Where there are floods, the water covers roads and paths. Cars and people can't get out of the area.

Discover!

Just 60 centimeters of water can make a car float!

The water goes into houses, and people have to leave their homes. Sometimes they have to get on the roof of their house to wait for help. Cars and people can't get into the area to help. The police and firefighters rescue people with boats and helicopters.

Floods can be very dangerous. The water moves fast and it's very strong. Don't play in flood water!

Go to pages 40–41 for activities.

10 Save Water!

When there is no water, rivers and lakes become dry. Plants can't grow and animals can't drink. If there is no food and no water to drink, people die, too. Water is very important. We all need to save water.

You can save water at home. Turn off the water when you brush your teeth. Take a shower, not a bath. You can also save water outside the home. Collect rainwater to water plants. Don't throw things into rivers or lakes. People and animals need clean water, not dirty water.

Remember! Our Earth needs water. People, animals, and plants need water. Save our wonderful water!

→ Go to pages 42–43 for activities.

1 Salt Water

← Read pages 4–5.

1 Write *Sea* or *Ocean*.

1 Atlantic _Ocean_

2 Pacific _____

3 Dead _____

4 Southern _____

5 South China _____

6 Indian _____

7 Arctic _____

8 Marmara _____

2 Write the numbers.

70 ~~5~~ 15 156 3 30 11,000

1 There are ___5___ oceans.

2 The Dead Sea is _____ % salt.

3 The South China Sea is _____ million square kilometers.

4 _____ % of Earth is covered with water.

5 The Pacific Ocean is _____ million square kilometers.

6 The Pacific Ocean is _____ times bigger than the USA.

7 The Marmara Sea is _____ square kilometers.

3 Write the words.

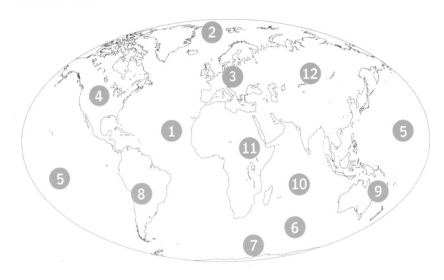

	1	Atlantic Ocean			_____
		_____			_____
		_____			_____
		_____			_____
		_____			_____
		_____			_____

4 Where do you live? Draw ★ on the map.

I live in _____

2 Fresh Water

← Read pages 6–7.

1 Write *true* or *false*.

1 30% of Earth's water is fresh water. _false_

2 Some of the fresh water is in the ocean. _____

3 Some of the fresh water is ice. _____

4 The longest river in the world is in North America. _____

5 Some fresh water is in clouds and rain. _____

6 We can drink all the water on Earth. _____

2 Find and write the words.

1 _glacier_

2 _____

g	l	a	c	i	e	r
b	a	d	a	e	f	i
c	k	h	v	g	o	v
a	e	i	e	r	u	e
b	s	r	a	i	n	r
s	o	i	l	j	l	a
e	t	c	l	o	u	d

5 _____

6 _____

3 _____

4 _____

7 _____

3 Complete the sentences.

1
Some of Earth's fresh
water _is in glaciers_ .

2 Some of the water is

_____ .

3
Some of the water

_____ .

4 Some of the _____

_____ .

5
Some of _____

_____ .

6 Some _____

_____ .

3 The Water Cycle

← Read pages 8–9.

1 Circle the correct words.

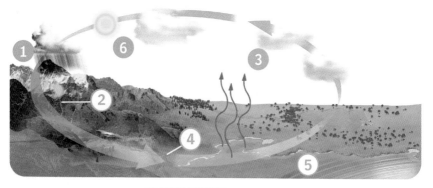

1 evaporation / (precipitation)   4 river / stream

2 river / stream   5 ocean / river

3 precipitation / evaporation   6 moon / sun

2 Number the sentences in order.

☐ It rains again.

☐ River water goes into the ocean.

[1] It rains.

☐ The water goes up into the sky and makes clouds.

☐ Rainwater goes into streams.

☐ It's sunny and the ocean gets warm.

☐ Stream water goes into rivers.

3 Follow the water. Write the words.

reservoir   home   dirty water   pipe   clean water

1 _____

2 _____

4 _____

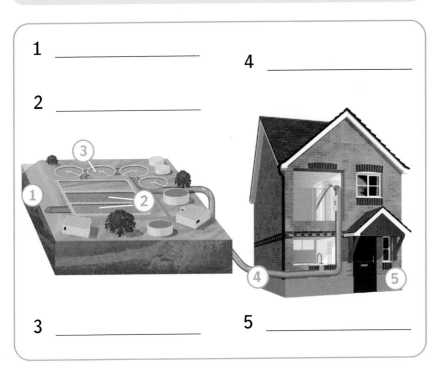

3 _____

5 _____

4 Write *true* or *false*.

1 The water we use comes from rivers
and reservoirs. _____

2 The water in the reservoir is too dirty
to drink. _____

3 Dirty water goes through pipes to
our homes. _____

4 Everybody has clean water at home. _____

4 Water at Home

← Read pages 10–11.

1 Which activities use water? Write ✔ or ✗.

2 Look at the picture. Complete the sentences.

> I wash   shower   I drink   my teeth   ~~the toilet~~
> television   I cook   I read   some water   I brush
> dressed   my hair   a comic book   the dishes

1 I flush _the toilet_ .

2 I take a _____.

3 _____ _____.

4 I get _____.

5 I brush _____.

6 _____ _____.

7 _____ _____.

8 I watch _____.

9 _____.

10 _____ _____.

3 **Write the numbers.**   9   27   80

1 We use _____ liters of water to take a shower.

2 We use _____ liters of water to take a bath.

3 We use _____ liters of water to flush the toilet.

4 **What do you use water for? Draw and write.**

5 Water Activities

← Read pages 12–13.

1 Find and write the words.

 1 _____

 2 _____

 3 _____

 4 _____

 5 _____

 6 _____

v	v	e	g	e	t	a	b
e	a	m	e	n	a	n	l
g	r	p	l	g	m	t	a
e	a	n	i	m	a	l	s
t	f	o	p	a	d	t	o
a	r	i	c	b	h	e	m
b	u	l	l	o	b	o	e
l	i	g	l	a	o	c	a
e	t	r	e	t	a	g	t
s	h	i	p	p	e	h	l

2 Match.

1 Animals

2 Fruit and vegetables need

3 People travel

4 Hydroelectricity

water to grow.

is electricity made from water.

drink water.

by boat and by ship.

3 Circle the correct words. Then complete the chart.

1 waterskiing / swimming

2 surfing / horse riding

3 diving / sailing

4 sailing / swimming

5 tennis / waterskiing

6 sailing / surfing

7 soccer / diving

8 surfing / sailing

Water Sports	Other Sports
_____	_____
_____	_____
_____	_____
_____	_____
_____	_____

6 We Need Water

← Read pages 14–15.

1 Write the words.

brain
bones
lungs
kidneys
blood

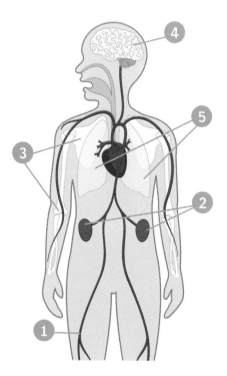

1 _____

2 _____

3 _____

4 _____

5 _____

2 Write *brain, bones,* or *blood.*

1 85% of our _____ is water.

2 Our _____ takes food to different parts of the body.

3 33% of our _____ is water.

4 If we're dehydrated, our _____ doesn't work.

3 Write the numbers. 4 3 70 8

1 About _____ % of our body is water.

2 We can live for _____ weeks without food.

3 We can't live for more than _____ days without water.

4 We need to drink _____ glasses of water every day.

4 Match.

1
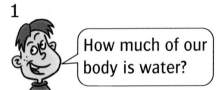 How much of our body is water?

 Three days.

2
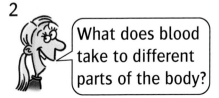 What does blood take to different parts of the body?

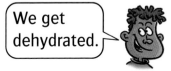 We get dehydrated.

3
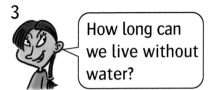 How long can we live without water?

 Oxygen and food.

4
 What happens if we don't drink water?

 About 70%.

7 Ocean Animals

← Read pages 16–17.

1 Write *true* or *false*.

1 The water in seas and oceans is salt water. _____

2 The blue whale lives in the ocean. _____

3 Sharks are the biggest ocean animals. _____

4 Fish need oxygen. _____

5 Jellyfish have skeletons. _____

6 An elephant is bigger than a blue whale. _____

2 Complete the sentences.

> ocean animals   biggest   big
> oceans   elephants   meters

The blue whale is the

_____ ocean animal.

It can be more than

30_____ long.

It can be as _____ as 25 _____.

It eats lots of little _____.

Blue whales live in most _____.

3 **What does water give ocean animals? Write.**

1 f ___ ___ ___

2 o ___ y ___ ___ ___

3 s ___ p ___ ___ ___ ___

4 **Draw and write about two ocean animals.**

This is a _____

_____

It lives in _____

_____

Water gives this animal _____

and _____

_____

_____

_____

_____

_____

_____

_____

_____

8 Other Animals

← Read pages 18–19.

1 Circle ◯ animals that live in fresh water and ◯ animals that live in salt water.

| duck | jellyfish | whale | frog |

| shark | crocodile | beaver | hippo |

2 **Complete the chart.**

Freshwater Animals	Saltwater Animals

3 **Match.**

1 Nile crocodiles	are land animals.
2 Zebras	need water to keep their skin healthy.
3 Hippos	eat other animals under water.

4 **Draw and write about a land animal that you like.**

This is a _____

It lives in _____

It eats _____

It drinks _____

I like it because _____

_____

_____

9 Too Much Water

← Read pages 20–21.

1 Circle the correct words.

1 Floods happen when there is **too much rain** / **no rain**.

2 People need to **leave** / **go into** their homes.

3 The police rescue people with **cars and bicycles** / **boats and helicopters**.

4 **Play** / **Don't play** in flood water!

2 Complete the puzzle. Write the secret word.

1 → | r | o | o | f |
2 →
3 →
4 →
5 →
6 →

The secret word is:

4 Color the picture and write the words.

1 _____ 6 _____

2 _____ 7 _____

3 _____ 8 _____

4 _____ 9 _____

5 _____ 10 _____

10 Save Water!

← Read pages 22–23.

1 Write ✔ or ✗.

Don't turn off the water.

Turn off the water.

Take a shower.

Take a bath.

Collect rainwater.

Don't collect rainwater.

Don't throw things
into rivers.

Throw things
into rivers.

2 **Design a poster. Write about how to save water.**

Save Water!

My Water Diary

1 **Keep a water diary for one day. Write ✔ every time you use water.**

		Total

2 **Write.**

In one day, I drink _____ glasses of

water. I flush the toilet _____ times.

I take _____ showers. I take

_____ baths. I brush my teeth

_____ times.

Water in My Country

1 Write the names of some rivers, lakes, seas, and oceans in or near your country.

Rivers	Lakes	Seas	Oceans

2 Draw and color a map of your country. Write the names of some rivers, lakes, seas, and oceans.

Picture Dictionary

 beaver

 cave

 clean

 clothes

 dirty

 dishes

 diving

 electricity

 flood

 flush

 food

 fruit

 glacier

 glass

 ground

 grow

 ice

 lake

 million

 ocean

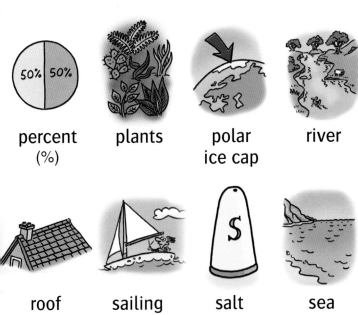

percent
(%)

plants

polar
ice cap

river

rocks

roof

sailing

salt

sea

ship

shower

skeleton

skin

soil

square
kilometer

stream

sunburnt

vegetables

waterskiing

waves

Oxford Read and Discover

Series Editor: Hazel Geatches • CLIL Adviser: John Clegg

Oxford Read and Discover graded readers are at six levels, for students from age 6 and older. They cover many topics within three subject areas, and support English across the curriculum, or Content and Language Integrated Learning (CLIL).

Available for each reader:
- Audio Pack
- Activity Book

Available for selected readers:
- e-Books

Teaching notes & CLIL guidance: **www.oup.com/elt/teacher/readanddiscover**

Subject Area / Level	The World of Science & Technology	The Natural World	The World of Arts & Social Studies
1 300 headwords	• Eyes • Fruit • Trees • Wheels	• At the Beach • In the Sky • Wild Cats • Young Animals	• Art • Schools
2 450 headwords	• Electricity • Plastic • Sunny and Rainy • Your Body	• Camouflage • Earth • Farms • In the Mountains	• Cities • Jobs
3 600 headwords	• How We Make Products • Sound and Music • Super Structures • Your Five Senses	• Amazing Minibeasts • Animals in the Air • Life in Rainforests • Wonderful Water	• Festivals Around the World • Free Time Around the World
4 750 headwords	• All About Plants • How to Stay Healthy • Machines Then and Now • Why We Recycle	• All About Desert Life • All About Ocean Life • Animals at Night • Incredible Earth	• Animals in Art • Wonders of the Past
5 900 headwords	• Materials to Products • Medicine Then and Now • Transportation Then and Now • Wild Weather	• All About Islands • Animal Life Cycles • Exploring Our World • Great Migrations	• Homes Around the World • Our World in Art
6 1,050 headwords	• Cells and Microbes • Clothes Then and Now • Incredible Energy • Your Amazing Body	• All About Space • Caring for Our Planet • Earth Then and Now • Wonderful Ecosystems	• Food Around the World • Helping Around the World